THE

PRINCESS OF BAGDAD.

ACT I.

A large and very elegant drawing-room, looking out on a garden. French window with balcony at the lower extremity to the right. To the left a conservatory. To the right a door opening into the apartment of LIONNETTE. *To the left a door opening into the apartment of* JOHN.

SCENE I.

RICHARD, THE FOOTMAN; afterwards JOHN and LIONNETTE.

THE FOOTMAN (*to* RICHARD, *who waits sitting near a table, turning over some papers.*)

The Count de Hun is here.

JOHN *enters; the* FOOTMAN *goes out.*

JOHN.

I am quite at your service, Master Richard, but I regret that you have inconvenienced yourself to come.

RICHARD.

Not at all; I live about two steps from here, and every evening, after my dinner, I take a short walk. Only, I am in a frock-coat, and you have friends.

JOHN.

Men only, some club friends. Lionnette is with them in the conservatory.

RICHARD.

Muster all the courage of which you are master.

JOHN.

We are ruined?

RICHARD.

Yes.

JOHN.

Poor Lionnette!

RICHARD.

Alas! It is a little her fault.

JOHN.

It is the fault of her mother, who reared her in luxury and without order. It is my fault, too, who was not as rich as my love; who not only never knew how to refuse her anything, but who did not even allow her time to wish for it; who told her to buy whatever she might wish for.

RICHARD.

And who also gave her by power of attorney—serious imprudence!—the right of buying, selling, of disposing of her property, and, in consequence, of yours, as it seemed fit to her. You owe one million, a hundred and seven thousand, one hundred and twenty-seven francs, fifty-two centimes. When I say, you owe, that is a figure of speech; your wife owes. In that amount there are only thirty-eight thousand francs of your own personal debts, and for which personally you have to be responsible, as you were married under the system of "separation of property."

JOHN.

I authorised my wife to make debts, these debts then are mine. In other words, as she has no money, it is I who have to pay. What are my assets?

RICHARD.

There is this house in which we are, which is worth eight hundred thousand francs when one does not want to sell it, but which would be worth from five hundred and fifty to five hundred and eighty thousand, the moment one is obliged to part with it; it is mortgaged for four hundred and fifty thousand francs.... Then there are the horses, the furniture, the laces, the jewels....

JOHN.

Very few jewels. A year ago Lionnette sold every jewel she had, with that heedlessness, that lightness of disposition, and that want of consideration, which are the basis of her character, and which you so well know.

RICHARD.

Ah! well, when you have sold all that you can possibly sell, there will remain about four hundred thousand francs.

JOHN.

Of capital?

RICHARD.

Of debts.

JOHN.

And the entail of my property?

RICHARD.

Ten thousand pounds income, inalienable, and all in your own power, fortunately.

JOHN.

Is it impossible to realize the capital?

RICHARD.

Utterly impossible. Your uncle foresaw what has happened, and, with the knowledge of your habits and the wishes of your mother, he was anxious to preserve to you always a crust of bread. There remains your sister.

JOHN (*with a doubtful tone*).

Yes, my sister!

RICHARD.

When you were married seven years ago, you know under what conditions, you had nothing more than what remained to you of the fortune of your father, about eight or nine hundred thousand francs. You made some legal interpellations against your mother in order to marry Lionnette—I call your wife Lionnette quite unceremoniously, as I knew her from her birth,—and your mother, even in her dying hour, did not pardon you. She has looked well after your sister's interest, and out of the 6,000,000 that she had she has left you only two, of which half went to pay the debts that you had already incurred. Your mother was a woman of clear perception....

JOHN.

Yes; but she ought to have understood....

RICHARD.

It is not easy to understand or to excuse that which wounds us in our tenderest feelings and in our most sacred traditions. The Countess of Hun, your mother, was entirely against the marriage you made. She knew you to be a man led by a first impression, incapable of resisting the first impulse. These tendencies are dangerous, not only for him who has them, but also for those who surround him. My age authorizes me to speak in this way to you. Your mother has only done, then, what every prudent judicious mother, loving her son, would have done in her place. In spite of everything, you married Mademoiselle de Quansas. I do not say that you were wrong; I simply make, as a lawyer and friend, the summary of a moral and legal position, and, in face of the present difficulties, I try to find out what we can obtain from it. Your sister is married, and to a husband who is head of the community. She has five children; an inheritance invested at interest, the portion which ought to come back to you having been left and allotted by your mother to the minor children; your mother made your sister swear never to alter her disposition of the property. These are all excellent reasons for keeping her brother's money. I am a lawyer; I understand these legitimate scruples of conscience!

JOHN.

I start to-morrow for Rennes. I shall go to see my sister; she will yield, perhaps, for the honour of our name.

RICHARD.

That name is no longer her's.

JOHN.

Nevertheless, I will try.

RICHARD.

Let us hope, but do not rely upon it. Your wife also had hope to the last, and has made a last effort among the family of ... her father: she has failed.

JOHN.

Yes.

RICHARD.

There is still another plan.

JOHN.

And that is?

RICHARD.

Call your creditors together, and offer them so much per cent.

JOHN.

Never.

LIONNETTE (*who enters during these last words*).

Never! If we have a sum larger than or equal to our debts, we must pay them fully; if we have only a smaller amount, we must give it to them on account, and look for means to procure the remainder; if we are not able to do it, then we have robbed all these confiding tradesmen, and there is but one thing left for my husband and me to do, that is, to shut ourselves up in a room hermetically sealed, set light to a pan of charcoal, and die together.

JOHN (*kissing her hands*).

I adore you.

RICHARD.

Yes, it is very fine, but like a drama or a romance, it is not reality.

LIONNETTE.

On the contrary, it is the most simple thing in the world—for me, at least. Either life, with all it is able to bestow, or death, with all it can promise; I understand nothing else. Do you think that after living as I have done, at my age I am going to allow myself to live in a garret, to go to market, and to reckon accounts with the laundress and general servant? It is unnecessary to try, I could never do it. Hunting-hound, shepherd-dog, if you like; blind-beggar's dog, never!

RICHARD.

And your son?

LIONNETTE.

My son, I would not have him die with us, it is very evident. But my son is six years old; he could still be brought up otherwise than I was. One could instil in him habits of work, and ordinary tastes, that I never had. There are 10,000 francs income from his father and the heirship inalienable; it would be misery for us, but independence for him. Men have no want of money, they only want it for their wives. It will be his duty not to love a prodigal like myself, and perhaps our example will be a warning for him.

RICHARD.

Very well. Now that we have well talked over, or rather you have well talked over, the useless and senseless, let us speak about the possible. Is it long since you have seen the Baroness de Spadetta?

LIONNETTE.

I see women as little as possible, my dear Richard, as you know well. Those who would come to me, I do not wish to see; others have had an air of making me feel their visits too great an honour. Let them stay at home; every one is free. Women, besides, are for other women nothing but enemies or accomplices. As to enemies, I have enough of them out-of-doors, without attracting them to my house; as to accomplices, I have not yet required any, and I hope to continue so. I content myself with the society of men; at least with them one knows what to adhere to, one knows quite well what they desire. But as to Madame Spadetta, that speaks for itself: she robbed me, and I turned her out, or nearly so. In any case, I want to see her no more.

RICHARD.

She robbed you! In what way?

LIONNETTE.

She knew my mother from my infancy: she was sometimes the mediator of my mother and myself with my father on matters of business, as she occupied an important place about him. A short time before his death my father said to me, "If I should die, Madame de Spadetta will remit you 1,500,000 francs." My father could leave me nothing in an official and public will, but he was incapable of telling me a thing like that if it were not true. There was left to Madame de Spadetta 2,000,000, with this note: "I am sure that Madame de Spadetta will make good use of that sum." It is clear. She kept the whole; it was easy to do.

JOHN.

You have never spoken to me of that.

LIONNETTE.

What good would it have done?

JOHN.

Have you claimed that amount from her?

LIONNETTE.

Certainly. She denied it.

JOHN (*to* RICHARD).

You might follow it up.

RICHARD.

No; it is trust-money. The law does not recognize it, and besides....

LIONNETTE.

I have only my word to support what I say. Madame de Spadetta replied to me that what my father had left her was in remuneration for services that her husband and she had rendered my father for thirty years. The truth is, that out of these two millions there were five hundred thousand francs for what she calls her services, and fifteen hundred thousand francs for me. It is for that that I turned her out of doors.

RICHARD.

Knowing that I have the care of your affairs, she came to find me out....

LIONNETTE.

To....

RICHARD.

To offer you five hundred thousand francs.

LIONNETTE.

On the part of whom? for she is a person equal to any kind of embassy.

RICHARD.

On the part of your father's family.

LIONNETTE.

What does she demand in return?...

RICHARD.

The giving up....

LIONNETTE.

Of all my father's letters.

RICHARD.

Yes; you knew it?

LIONNETTE.

I suspected it, from a few words she said to me. I refuse to do so.

RICHARD.

Your mother, before she died, handed over, for a much less important amount, all the letters that she also possessed from your father.

LIONNETTE.

My mother did as she pleased; I, too, shall do as I please; and, as my mother is dead, I refrain from saying all I think.

RICHARD.

Why do you care so much about those letters?

LIONNETTE.

You ask me that, Mr. Richard? Why do I care so much for the letters of a father whom I loved, who loved me, the man who was my father, and who is dead?

RICHARD.

What do you intend to do with them?

LIONNETTE.

To keep them, to read them over again, as I do now from time to time, when the living trouble or disgust me; and when I die, carry them with me and give them back to him—to him—if it be true that one meets again in death those one has loved in life. Who knows? Perhaps, after being so powerful on earth, he will have no one but me in heaven. So I must keep something by which he may know me—up there—since he was not able to recognize me here below.

JOHN (*to* RICHARD).

How can one help worshipping that woman? (*He takes her head between his hands and kisses her hair.*) There.

RICHARD (*taking the hand of* LIONNETTE).

The fact is that she has the blood of a good race in her, and that they named you very appropriately, calling you Lionnette—little lioness; but unfortunately it is not with that that creditors are paid, and I offer you the only way which is open to you.

LIONNETTE.

God has hitherto given, God will give again; if He forget us, then chance must take us.

Scene II.

GODLER, NOURVADY, TRÉVELÉ.

TRÉVELÉ (*going towards* LIONNETTE.)

Tell me, Countess, are we, yes or no, Godler the ever youthful, Nourvady the ever grave, and I, Trévelé, the ever jesting—are we, yes or no, invited by you, Countess, the ever beautiful, and by your husband, the ever blissful (it would be difficult for him to be otherwise)—are we, yes or no, invited to dine at your table and to spend the evening with you afterwards?

LIONNETTE.

Yes.

TRÉVELÉ.

Then, lovely countess, permit me to observe that you are never where we are. Kindly give us information. When one sees you one loves you; but when one loves you where does one see you?

LIONNETTE (*smiling*).

Here.

TRÉVELÉ.

We supposed so, but it is now two hours since....

LIONNETTE.

Oh! not two hours!

TRÉVELÉ.

Three hours ago you forsook us in the middle of the conservatory. First, a domestic came to look for the count; we accepted that affliction: but, in your turn, you disappeared without even troubling any one to come and look for you. Well, we are all three charming—Godler, Nourvady, and I; it is difficult to find three more delightful and witty men, but we have such a habit of seeing each other that we do not enjoy ourselves at all when we are by ourselves. So if, after having us for seven hours, you discover you have had enough of us, tell us so without ceremony. We are going to drive back to the club, where we shall have a good game of baccarat; we will try, Godler and I, to win a hundred thousand francs from that millionaire Nourvady;—that will make him cheerful, perhaps.

LIONNETTE.

Gentlemen, I offer you every excuse. It was on account of a most important and unforeseen affair. (*She presents* RICHARD.) Master Richard, solicitor, an old friend of mine. (*She introduces the gentlemen.*) Mr. de Trévelé, Mr. Godler, Mr. Nourvady. (*The gentlemen bow.*) And now, to strengthen you after all your fatigue and trouble, I am going to offer you a cup of tea, iced coffee, or chocolate.

(*She approaches the table, upon which, during this discourse, the servants have put the articles mentioned.*)

RAOUL (*entering with his nurse, who remains near the door, and going to his mother*).

Mamma!

LIONNETTE.

Gentlemen, here is my son, whom I beg to present to you. Bow, Raoul.

(RAOUL *bows already like a man of the world, putting his heels together and bending his head*; TRÉVELÉ *and* GODLER *kiss him*; NOURVADY *kisses his hand, after hesitating a moment*; RAOUL *goes back to his mother, who kisses him, putting her arm round his neck.*)

RAOUL.

Take care, you will crumple my collar.

LIONNETTE.

I beg your pardon, I wanted to kiss you. You don't love me, then?

RAOUL.

Oh, yes, I love you very much.

LIONNETTE.

Then you are going to help me pour out the tea?

RAOUL.

No; I came to ask not to go to bed yet. I should prefer to play with Jane's little nephew, who has come with his mother to see her, but she will not let me without your permission.

LIONNETTE.

Very well, I give you leave. Run away now, my child.

RAOUL.

Good bye. (*He goes away running.*)

LIONNETTE.

And you go away like that? (RAOUL *bows again, and wants to go away.* LIONNETTE *shows him* RICHARD.) And Mr. Richard? And your father, too?

(*At each name mentioned* RAOUL *passes to the person, who kisses him. One can see he is in a great hurry to run away. When he gets to* JOHN, *the latter takes him in his arms and kisses him very warmly.*)

JOHN.

Don't be afraid, I am not going to crumple your collar. (*He puts the child on the ground again, who tries afresh to escape.*)

LIONNETTE (*who during this time is serving the tea*).

And me, Raoul.

(RAOUL *runs back again and kisses his mother.*)

LIONNETTE (*with a sigh*).

Go and play, my child, go; and amuse yourself well.

(LIONNETTE, *a cup in each hand, presents one to* GODLER, *the other to* TRÉVELÉ.)

GODLER (*touching* LIONNETTE's *hand with his lips*).

Dare I be so bold?

LIONNETTE.

If you wish it.

TRÉVELÉ.

And I?

LIONNETTE.

And you, too. Only, take the cups, or you will burn my hands with the tea.

GODLER.

And you, Nourvady?

NOURVADY.

Thank you, I ask for nothing, not even a cup of tea.

(JOHN *chats with* RICHARD *in a corner*.)

TRÉVELÉ.

And the Countess will be right never to give you anything. People who ask nothing are often those who wish too much. Under cover of forty millions....

NOURVADY.

My money has nothing to do with this.

TRÉVELÉ.

Certainly not; but all the same, when one has forty millions one finds a great many things easier than when one has, like me, only one. Ah, well, I must say, to the credit of Nourvady, it is in vain that he has two millions income at least—because he is a man who makes the best of his capital. He is, after all, the most sentimental of us three, and who takes love most seriously. He is a millionaire Anthony, and in our time it is remarkable.

GODLER.

And useful.

(RICHARD *and* JOHN, *who have chatted in a corner of the drawing-room, make their way to the terrace, where they chat in sight of the public.*)

NOURVADY.

I do not know why Trévelé always assails me on the score of my fortune, of which I talk as little as possible. I am rich, but it is through no fault of mine. If that had depended on me alone, it certainly would never have happened. I am not clever enough to make forty millions. Fortunately, I had a father who was very intelligent, and, at the same time, very honourable. This father had a large bank at Vienna, which was very prosperous. He died, leaving me forty millions. It was, therefore, necessary to resign myself to accept them.

LIONNETTE.

Easy resignation, I think, and that I should have had like you.

NOURVADY.

Ah! Madam, a fortune is a burden like anything else, at least for a man, for women have more grace and intelligence in spending money than we. But with much simplicity, a few efforts of the intellect, a little ingenuity in the way of rendering services—there is sometimes a way to get out of the difficulty—for a man.

TRÉVELÉ.

And you get out of it remarkably well, my dear fellow! If we tease you about your millions, it is because it is the only subject we can joke you upon.

NOURVADY (*holding out his hand to him*).

Rest assured, my dear Trévelé, that I am never offended at your jokes.

GODLER (*to* TRÉVELÉ).

It is very fortunate for you, for if Nourvady were at all susceptible you would have a nice time.

TRÉVELÉ.

Why?

GODLER.

Because he kills a bird at every shot.

TRÉVELÉ.

But I am not a bird.

GODLER.

And he hits the mark eleven times out of twelve, and barely escapes the twelfth.

NOURVADY.

Fortunately I have an easy temper, which I have acquired by self-control, for I was naturally violent and irritable.

GODLER.

That poor Marnepont discovered something of that.

NOURVADY.

Don't let us speak of that.

LIONNETTE.

Oh, yes, please let us speak of it. I knew Mr. de Marnepont very well, and I have heard in fact that he was killed. By you, then?

NOURVADY.

Alas! yes, madam.

LIONNETTE.

In a duel?

NOURVADY.

Certainly. I did not assassinate him.

LIONNETTE.

He was very annoying.

NOURVADY.

That was not the only reason of his death. He had other defects. He was insolent, and, above all, a liar.

LIONNETTE.

What insolence was he guilty of? What lie did he tell? I will wager there was a woman in the case.

(RICHARD *is gone*. JOHN *hears all that is said, leaning upon the back of the couch where his wife is sitting*.)

NOURVADY.

No, madam, it concerned me pitifully. Mr. de Marnepont calumniated me. He said I was hump-backed, which is not true. I have only the left shoulder a little higher than the right.

LIONNETTE.

That is not seen at all.

NOURVADY.

It is not seen any longer, especially since that duel. In any case, no one says any more about it. My father, it is true, had a round back—at the close of his life principally. He had worked hard, stooping over a desk. That makes one round-shouldered in the end. Poor father! he said to me: "You have one shoulder higher than the other, the left; you get that from me; I ask your pardon for it, and I will endeavour to leave you what will make you forget it. But there are some people who will mock much more willingly at you as you will be very rich. Be strong in all sword-play, then; that will equalize everything." I followed the advice of my father, and I am astonished at the result. Then, as Mr. de Marnepont was a very good shot, I chose the pistol as our weapon. I was affronted, so wished to show him what good play was. We were allowed to fire at will; he fired first, and lodged a ball in my right shoulder, which naturally made me make this movement (*he raises his right shoulder a little*), for it was very painful, and I suffer from it often still. There are some days when my right arm is as if paralyzed. Whoever would get the better of me if I affronted him, has only to choose the sword; I should probably be killed at the second thrust.

TRÉVELÉ.

And Marnepont?

NOURVADY.

Ah, well! In making the movement occasioned by the pain, this shoulder was for the moment higher than that. (*He raises the right arm a little.*) "Ah, said my opponent, laughing, I made a mistake, it is the right which is highest." It was not bad—for him, but it was bad taste. Then I fired. It was the first time that poor fellow showed any wit; he wasn't used to it; it killed him.

GODLER (*quite low to* TRÉVELÉ).

He wants to rise in the estimation of our hostess; he is a clever fellow.

LIONNETTE (*looking at* NOURVADY, *who is going towards* GODLER *and* TRÉVELÉ, *one sitting and the other standing at the other side of the room*).

He is peculiar, that man.

JOHN.

Do you find him odd?

LIONNETTE.

Yes, he is so unlike any one else.

JOHN.

Indeed?

LIONNETTE.

What is the matter with you? What are you thinking about?

JOHN.

I am thinking that that odd man is very happy.

LIONNETTE.

In having the left shoulder higher than the right, and a ball in the latter?

JOHN.

In having what I have not, in having forty millions.

LIONNETTE.

Ah, yes, that would help us out of our difficulties.

JOHN.

My poor Lionnette, I am very unhappy.

LIONNETTE.

Why?

JOHN.

Because I am not able to give you any longer what I formerly gave you.

LIONNETTE.

I shall do very well without it.

JOHN.

You are incapable of it; you said it yourself just now.

LIONNETTE.

There are moments when I no longer know what I say; you must not pay attention to it. Chance has done much for me in my life; it may still find a way.

JOHN.

And if chance gets tired, and if you also get as tired? I shall never say—"if you love me no more;" in your heart you have never loved me.

LIONNETTE.

Why did I marry you, then?

JOHN.

Because your mother advised you to do it.

LIONNETTE.

It is perhaps the only good advice she ever gave me, and I assure you I have been very grateful for what you have done for me.

JOHN.

Gratitude is not love.

LIONNETTE.

Love comes afterwards.

JOHN.

A long time afterwards, for it has not come yet.

LIONNETTE.

The most beautiful creature in the world could not give more than she has. I have given all I had to give. Is it love? Is it not love? I know not. I have no line of comparison, never having given to any one but you.

(*She hesitates a moment before continuing.*)

JOHN.

You were going to say something else.

LIONNETTE.

No.

JOHN.

Yes. Say it, whatever it was.

(*He draws* LIONNETTE *by the hand, close to him.*)

GODLER.

There are the plots beginning again. An odd kind of a house this.

(*The three persons go out on the terrace, and from there into the garden, where one sees no more of them.*)

LIONNETTE.

I was going to say that perhaps you find that I do not love you enough, because you love me too much. Then you have been much too good to me; you have done whatever I wished; you did wrong. You should have been more my master, in order to counterbalance the bad influence of my mother, to change my habits, to offer more resistance, and to save me from myself.

JOHN.

To save you? What have you done then?

LIONNETTE.

I have ruined you.

JOHN.

That is all.

LIONNETTE.

It is quite enough.

JOHN.

You have never thought of....

LIONNETTE.

Of what?

JOHN.

Of another?

LIONNETTE (*laughing*).

You are mad. You have always been a little inclined that way. It is true that if you had not been silly you would never have married me.

JOHN.

Whether I am mad or not, answer my question.

LIONNETTE.

No, you can be assured on that point. I have never thought of any one else.

JOHN.

And if I were to die; if I killed myself; if you, in the end, became a widow, and that man who is there—that strange man, that millionaire—made you an offer, would you marry him?

LIONNETTE.

We have not arrived at that yet.

JOHN.

Who can tell? In the meantime that man loves you, and wishes to go so far as to make you love him without waiting for my death. You have remarked it as well as I.

LIONNETTE.

Where is the woman who does not discover such things? Ask those who have never, by anyone, been told or allowed to see that they were loved, what they think of life. Our dream is to hear such declarations; our art is to listen to them; and our genius and power not to believe in them.

JOHN.

Has he declared himself?

LIONNETTE.

Never.

JOHN.

Your word for it.

LIONNETTE.

My word of honour.

JOHN.

It will come to that.

LIONNETTE.

He will not be the last, I hope. What do you want to make of it?

JOHN.

He will declare himself, perhaps, at the moment when nothing remains for you but misery or suicide: both are equally hard for a young and beautiful woman.

LIONNETTE (*seriously and haughtily*).

You are confounding me with some other woman whom you loved before me. Do I expose myself to these suppositions by my ways of living? Ah! no, no. I have many defects but no vices, I believe; and, in spite of my anxiety for the future, I have never yet dreamed of these ways of escape. I trust never to think for a moment of them.

JOHN.

How much I love you! You have in you all that is most strange and noble in this world. You have a power over me almost superhuman. I think of no one but you; I want nothing but you; I dream only of you. If I suspect, it is because I love you. When you are not here, I do not exist: when I find you again, I tremble like a child. I implore you never to trifle with that love,—so deep, and, yet, so troubled. I do not ask you to love me beyond your power of loving; but love none other more than me. You know not—I do not know myself—what the result might be. When I think of the future, I grow giddy. (*In a low, eager voice*) I adore you! I adore you!

(*During the last words* NOURVADY *has come on to the stage again. He has looked at* JOHN *and* LIONNETTE. *He takes his hat*; GODLER *and* TRÉVELÉ *follow him.*)

LIONNETTE.

Do not speak so low; you could be heard.

JOHN.

Kiss me, then.

LIONNETTE.

You wish me to kiss you. Here?

JOHN.

Here.

LIONNETTE.

Before everybody?

JOHN.

Before him.

LIONNETTE.

The same subject. Take care! You are doing him a great honour.

JOHN.

It is an idea that I have.

LIONNETTE.

You would like it?

JOHN.

Yes.

LIONNETTE.

You know well you must not dare me to anything.

JOHN.

I implore you.

LIONNETTE.

Once, twice, three times (*kissing him on both cheeks*). So much the worse for you. There!

GODLER (*laughing*.)

Ah! my friends, ah! You have decidedly a manner of your own of receiving.

THE SERVANT (*entering*).

Some one wants to see the Count.

GODLER.

Too late, my man, too late! He ought to have come a minute earlier.

THE SERVANT.

I beg your pardon, Sir?

GODLER.

Go, go! It would be too long to explain.

JOHN (*to the Servant*).

Who wants to see me?

THE SERVANT.

It is a clerk of Mr. Richard.

JOHN.

Very well, I will go to him. (*To* GODLER *and to* TRÉVELÉ) I am coming back immediately.

GODLER.

Don't study us.

(GODLER *and* TRÉVELÉ *accompany* JOHN *to the room at the end, where they remain some moments talking in sight of the public; and, when* JOHN *is gone away, they remain there, walking up and down, during the scene between* LIONNETTE *and* NOURVADY.)

NOURVADY (*goes towards* LIONNETTE, *hat in hand*).

Adieu, Countess.

LIONNETTE.

Are you going to leave us?

NOURVADY.

Yes, your house is in a visible agitation. There is less indiscretion in perceiving it than in remaining.

LIONNETTE.

When shall we see you again?

NOURVADY.

Never!

LIONNETTE.

You are going away?

NOURVADY.

No; but I shall come here no more.

LIONNETTE (*laughing*).

You did not enjoy your dinner?

NOURVADY.

Do me the honour of listening to me to the end.

GODLER (*to* TRÉVELÉ, *on seeing* LIONNETTE *seat herself again, and* NOURVADY *approach her*.)

That's well! With the other now.

NOURVADY.

I love you (LIONNETTE *makes a movement*). You know it; and you ought to have foreseen that I should one day tell you so.

LIONNETTE.

Yes; it is only five minutes ago that my husband and I were speaking about it.

NOURVADY.

Do not laugh. You may tell by the tone of my voice that I am very serious. I love you passionately. You do not love me; you do not even think of me. It is probable that you will never love me. I possess nothing of all the essentials to tempt a woman like yourself—except a fortune.

LIONNETTE (*rising to retire*).

Sir!

NOURVADY.

Have patience! I am not capable of failing in respect towards you, as I love you. You are ruined—irreparably ruined. You can accept, it is true, the proposals that Madame Spadetta has had made to you, and free yourself in that manner. There would be no longer debt, but there would be straitened circumstances, and, perhaps, misery. Without counting that, it would be a great grief for you to give up, for ever, certain letters; a grief that whoever loves you ought to spare you.

LIONNETTE (*re-seating herself*).

How do you know that?

NOURVADY.

With money one knows all one wants to know, especially when Madame Spadetta is able to furnish all the information one requires. Do you remember, Countess, that one day, some months ago, passing through the Champs Elysées with your husband and me, you remarked at No. 20 a private house that was nearly finished.

LIONNETTE.

Yes.

NOURVADY.

You admired then the exterior elegance of that house. That was sufficient to induce me to resolve that no man should inhabit it;—another time you might have looked mechanically in passing on that side, and the proprietor at his window might have imagined that it was at him the lovely Countess of Hun was looking. I have bought that house, and I have had it furnished as elegantly as possible. If, in a year, in two years, in ten years, if—to-morrow

—circumstances force you to sell this house where we are at this moment, think of that house in the Champs Elysées that no one has ever yet inhabited. The carriages are waiting in the coach-houses, the horses in the stables, the footmen in the ante-rooms. The little door that this key opens is only for you. (*He shows a little key.*) That door you will easily recognize: your monogram is on it. From the moment you cross it, if you cross the threshold one day, you will not even have the trouble of opening another with it; all the doors will be open in the way that leads to your apartment. In the drawing-room is an Arabian coffer of marvellous workmanship; this coffer contains a million in gold, struck on purpose for you: it is virgin gold, such as gold ought to be that your little hands deign to touch. You can make use of all in this coffer; when it is empty it will fill itself again—it is a secret. The deeds which confer upon you the ownership of this house are deposited in one of the cabinets in the drawing-room. You will have only to sign them whenever you may like legally to be the owner. Is it necessary to add that you owe nothing to anyone for all that, and that you will remain absolute mistress of your actions? To-morrow I shall pass the day in that house, to assure myself that all there is in a fit state to receive you; and I shall never appear there again until you tell me yourself to come—or to remain there.

(LIONNETTE *takes the key that* NOURVADY *has laid upon the table while talking; rises, and goes to throw it out of the open window; passes before* NOURVADY *in going to rejoin* GODLER *and* TRÉVELÉ.)

NOURVADY (*while she passes in front of him*).

That window looks upon your garden, Countess, not upon the street. In a garden a key can be picked up again.

(*He bows, and leaves her, to take his departure.*)

LIONNETTE (*in a low voice*).

The insolent fellow!

JANE (*entering, to* LIONNETTE).

Master Raoul will not go to bed, Madam.

LIONNETTE.

Very well; I am coming.
(*She goes out by the door from which* JANE *has spoken to her.*)

TRÉVELÉ (*to* GODLER).

Again running away! that is too strong. This time, let us go too.

NOURVADY.

No, remain; I think you will be wanted here. Good bye. (*He goes away.*)

SCENE III.

GODLER, TRÉVELÉ.

TRÉVELÉ (*to* GODLER, *while eating a cake*).

I assure you that Nourvady is a personage apart. Listen now; let us eat all the cakes, drink all the lemonade, and during that time you can solve the enigma, for at length you ought to know what is going on in this house, you who have always been a friend of the Marchioness of Quansas. It is said even....

GODLER (*after looking around him*).

In 1853.

TRÉVELÉ.

You are decided?

GODLER.

In 1853.

TRÉVELÉ.

Why did you never tell it?

GODLER.

In 1853 there was a Madam Duranton, who kept a shop in the rue Traversière.

TRÉVELÉ.

Where may the rue Traversière be?

GODLER.

It was a little cross street, of compromised fame, leading from the rue St. Honoré to the rue Richelieu. Madame Duranton, a widow—one could not be more a widow—sold left-off clothes. You can imagine the rest....

TRÉVELÉ.

Yes, I see, I see; make haste.

GODLER.

Madame Duranton, at whose house two or three friends and I went sometimes to pass the evening, and who gave us sometimes cider and chesnuts in her little back shop....

TRÉVELÉ.

In 1853?

GODLER.

In 1853.

TRÉVELÉ.

How old were you?

GODLER.

I was 39 years old.

TRÉVELÉ.

You are old, then?

GODLER.

I am 66.

TRÉVELÉ.

You don't look that age.

GODLER.

Because I get myself up very well.

TRÉVELÉ.

What a good fellow! Go on.

GODLER.

Would you like us to make a bet?

TRÉVELÉ.

No, you would gain it; Florimond has told it to me.

GODLER (*who is sitting down*).

Very well; go and shut the window, and give me something to drink.

TRÉVELÉ.

Go on.

GODLER.

Madame Duranton had a daughter.

TRÉVELÉ.

To whom you made love?

GODLER.

To whom we all made love, without any good intention—you can understand. The young girl, then between 18 and 19 years old, was a beautiful creature, with naturally golden hair, like women have artificially now-a-days, with violet-blue eyes, cheeks like a rose of Bengal, and teeth and lips resembling almonds between two halves of a cherry.

(*During this time* GODLER *from time to time arranges his whiskers, and a lock of hair which falls over his forehead, with a little comb that he takes out of his pocket.*)

TRÉVELÉ.

One could almost wish to taste thereof. You are a poet!

GODLER.

That I had from my youth. At that time....

TRÉVELÉ.

In your youth?

GODLER.

No, in 1853, there were a king and queen....

TRÉVELÉ.

Who reigned....

GODLER.

Exactly.

TRÉVELÉ.

Happy time! Where did they reign?

GODLER.

At Bagdad.

TRÉVELÉ.

Thank you.

GODLER.

This king and this queen had an only son, who was to succeed them. This son, 23 years old, took much too seriously his part of heir-presumptive. But what was the use of having a crown, if, in his turn, he was not to have an heir to leave it to? However, nothing in the young prince indicated the least inclination towards love, legitimate or otherwise.

TRÉVELÉ.

He was not like you.

GODLER.

No, he was not like me.

TRÉVELÉ.

Go on.

GODLER.

Always study; always reflection; always indifference.

TRÉVELÉ.

A strange prince!

GODLER.

The ambassadors opened negotiation upon negotiation uselessly with foreign courts in view of a political alliance. Several young princesses of surrounding countries, of Hindostan, of Persia, and even of Europe....

TRÉVELÉ.

How well you relate a thing!

GODLER.

Were waiting full-dressed, their hair well-dressed and splendidly perfumed, for the king of Bagdad to ask their hand for his son. The telegraph replied always: Wait! Wait!

TRÉVELÉ.

Go on quickly.

GODLER.

A chamberlain had a very simple idea.

TRÉVELÉ.

In general the ideas of chamberlains are very simple.

GODLER.

This was, to let the prince travel, in order that he might see other women than those of Bagdad, since they were acknowledged to be insufficient, and to send him at once to Paris.

TRÉVELÉ.

Bad complaints require strong remedies.

GODLER.

But this was not all; beauty was necessary, and it must be stock of a particular kind: also those that he did not marry must differ only in rank from the one he did marry. In fact, it was not a Lycœnion, but a perfect Chloe, that was sought for the instruction of this Daphnis, and it was not to be child's play.

TRÉVELÉ.

I see the young Lionnette dawning. But how did everything come about?

GODLER.

That will make the subject of the following chapter. The ambassador of Bagdad came with us sometimes in the evening, to eat chesnuts and drink cider at Madame Duranton's.

TRÉVELÉ.

And he discovered a way of leading the prince to eat the cherries and almonds?

GODLER.

Who acquired such a taste for these delicious fruits, that he wanted to eat nothing else, had no wish to go away, had no inclination whatever for study, no longer wished to reign—he wanted to marry. However, the king, informed and satisfied on the subject, recalled his son. He must go back to Bagdad. Daphnis wept, and Chloe also.

TRÉVELÉ.

You are king, you cry, and I depart.

GODLER.

And that is how the beautiful Lionnette came into the world; having for legal father a Marquis de Quansas, a ruined gentleman, rather a bad character, who turned up just at the right moment to lay his hand on a marriage portion, give his name to the mother and daughter, and die a short time after, without falling into the hands of the correctional police, as every one expected to see him do.

TRÉVELÉ.

Then the countess is daughter of a prince?

GODLER.

Daughter of a king, even—for the prince succeeded his father.

TRÉVELÉ.

What a strange country!

GODLER.

Daughter of a king and of an adventuress; daughter herself of no one knows who. From that comes, no doubt, the strangeness in the nature of Lionnette, whom we, who know the circumstances, named, when she was very young, the Princess of Bagdad. People never knew what it meant, but it is useless for all the world to know what some things mean.

TRÉVELÉ.

And the mother, the Marchioness of Quansas, has she seen the king again since that adventure?

GODLER.

Often, and for several years. Thence comes the great luxury and style of the house. But she became so badly-conducted, and abused so much the goodness of the king to her, that he—himself now become father of a large family, as everything led to hope after his return from Paris, and the marchioness no longer being young—lost all patience, and gave no more money, except to his daughter, whom he adored, and whom he saw in secret. But he died quite suddenly.

TRÉVELÉ.

I know whom you mean.

GODLER.

Then we both know it, that is sufficient. After the death of the king all the resources disappeared. Fortunately, the love and marriage of our friend John de Hun were found in the nick of time, to maintain for some time the importance of the house; but at this moment I think the downfall is not far off, and all these comings and goings of to-day may very well be the last signs of it. All the legitimate ways are exhausted; there remains nothing now but the others.

TRÉVELÉ.

Which are happily the most numerous. It costs too much for us, my poor old Godler. For the present it is just the affair of the gloomy millionaire: we shall see later on. There is nothing more to drink; they have quite forgotten us. Put your comb in your pocket again, your lock of hair is very well like that; now let us go away. A peculiar kind of a house. Where is my hat?

(*While they both look for their hats, their backs turned to the bottom of the room,* John *enters, very pale, and visibly affected.*)

Scene IV.

THE SAME PERSONS, JOHN.

John.

I beg your pardon, gentlemen, for having left you so long alone in my house, but I have been suddenly called away. I reckoned upon being back sooner. And....

(*He draws his hand across his forehead.*)

Godler.

You are suffering much?

John.

It is nothing.... A little fatigue, it is very warm.

Trévelé.

We are going away.

John.

However, it may be that I shall stand in need of two sure friends. Can I count upon you?

Trévelé (*aside*).

Nourvady was right.

Godler.

Certainly; we shall breakfast, Trévelé and I, to-morrow at 12 o'clock at the club. If you have anything to say to us.

John.

Thank you. Till to-morrow then.

Godler (*aside, as he goes out*).

Poor fellow.

Trévelé (*aside, as he goes out*).

The weather is getting stormy, as the sailors say.

Scene V.

John *alone at first, afterwards* Lionnette.

John, *standing alone, lays his hand on the top of a chair; then he pulls off his cravat and loosens the collar of his shirt, as if he were suffocating and wished to breathe more freely. He goes at length to the window, breathes the air strongly two or three times, and walks towards the door by which* Lionnette *went out*: Lionnette *enters by the same door when he is half-way towards it.*

John (*standing still*).

Where have you come from?

Lionnette.

I have just come from putting the child to bed, who was very disobedient this evening, and I came back to find the gentlemen again.

John.

They are all three gone.

Lionnette.

What is the matter with you? You are quite pale.... What has happened again?

John.

You want to know?

LIONNETTE.

Yes, certainly. I ask you to tell me.

JOHN (*walking up to her and putting his fist towards her face*).

When I think how I failed in respect for my mother, who died cursing me, and all for this creature.

LIONNETTE (*coming up to him*).

I do not understand.

JOHN.

You do not understand!

LIONNETTE.

No; I believe, I hope, that you are still madder than usual. What is it?

JOHN (*drawing some papers from his pocket*).

What is all this? It is this, that Mr. Nourvady has had all your debts paid. He had no wish to do me the honour of paying mine; but you, you owe nothing any more. That is what it is. Now do you understand?

LIONNETTE (*stupified*).

Mr. Nourvady!

JOHN.

Yes, Mr. Nourvady, your lover!

LIONNETTE (*indignantly*).

My lover!

JOHN.

Yes, your lover, to whom you have sold yourself and my name, your honour and mine, for some hundreds of thousands of francs. For your own honour it is too much, but for mine it is too little.

LIONNETTE.

Perhaps you will tell me what all this means?

JOHN.

Mr. Richard has just sent some one for me; on his return home this evening he found all the bills of your creditors sent back to him receipted, at the same time writing that they were all fully paid. By whom? You know well.

(*He throws the papers on the table.*)

LIONNETTE.

I swear to you....

JOHN (*mad with rage*).

'Tis false? 'Tis false! There was a way, painful for you, to free yourself; it was proposed to you at first; you obstinately rejected it.... You had your own reasons, it was useless! The contract was concluded and carried out. Since when, may I ask?

LIONNETTE.

Ah! when will you have finished insulting me! I tell you that of which you accuse me is not true. At present, if you do not believe me, do whatever you like.

JOHN (*exasperated*).

I turn you out of doors.

LIONNETTE.

Unfortunately, this house is mine, and I remain in it.

JOHN.

It is true; I beg your pardon! I forgot that your mother had foreseen all. This house, paid for by me, is yours, but the debts incurred by you are paid by some one else. It is a compensation. It is I who will leave this house, you may rest contented. I am going at once.... I am going to look for some money—at my sister's—it signifies not where. I must find some, even if I have to steal in my turn. And after that we shall see. Adieu!

(*He goes away with a menacing gesture.*)

LIONNETTE (*alone*).

Adieu! (*Shrugging her shoulders, and going towards her apartment.*) The idiot! (*She goes into her room.*)

ACT II.

A small drawing-room, in great taste, combined with much luxury. General arrangements of the room rather adapted for repose and sleep —for tête-à-tête—than for general conversation and reception. A closed iron coffer, containing the million which has been spoken of in the First Act, placed on a table.

At the rising of the curtain, the drawing-room is empty. The stage remains thus unoccupied for about a moment. A curtain screen lowered at the left of the spectator, also one equally lowered at the right. A large screen lowered at the back, and concealing, like the other two, a door that can be locked.

SCENE I.

LIONNETTE, *veiled, enters at the left; draws back the screen, stops, looks around her; goes slowly to the door at the back, which she opens and shuts again, after having looked in. Ten o'clock strikes. She goes and looks through the door at the right, then through the glass between the two rooms over the mantel-piece, and presses the knob of the electric bell, which is by the side of the chimney-piece. Silence reigns for a few seconds.* LIONNETTE, *astonished, looks around her.* NOURVADY *appears at the back of the room.*

SCENE II.

LIONNETTE, NOURVADY.

(NOURVADY *stops, after having let fall the screen, and salutes* LIONNETTE *very respectfully. He is hat in hand.*)

LIONNETTE (*troubled*).

Is it you?

NOURVADY.

You rang.

LIONNETTE.

I thought a footman would answer.

NOURVADY.

Your most grateful and humble slave has come.

LIONNETTE (*severely*).

You were waiting for me?

NOURVADY.

Yes.

LIONNETTE.

That is the reason you said yesterday that you would be in this house to-day.

NOURVADY.

Yes.

Lionnette.

You were sure that I should come.

Nourvady (*a little ironically*).

Sure. I only regret that you have had to take the trouble to go and look in your garden for the key that you threw there.

Lionnette.

The fact is that you have discovered the only way to compel me,—an infamous way, Sir. (*While speaking she has taken off the veils that covered her face, and thrown them on the table.*) You acknowledge, Sir, do you not, the infamous means you have adopted. Answer me!

Nourvady.

I have no answer. You are in your own house; I could if I wished withdraw myself from your insult and anger: but, apart from the fact that my courage to do so forsook me from the moment you came here, I am sure you have something else to say to me, and I remain to hear it.

Lionnette.

Truly, Sir, an explanation between you and me is necessary; and, as you did not wish to return to my house, I am come to seek it in yours. Besides, I like plain and open situations; and I do not fear, especially at this moment in my life, categorical explanations and undisguised expressions,—blunt even, if we can understand each other better in that way. I heard such things yesterday that my ears now can lend themselves to anything. An act such as yours—a step such as I have taken—an interview like this that we are having, and which may lead to results so positive and so serious—are so exceptional that words of double meaning could not explain them. (*Seating herself.*) I have not long known you; I have never attempted to attract you by the least coquetry; I have never asked anything of you; and you have just dishonoured me morally and socially without my being able to defend myself. It is remarkably clever. Whatever I may say, no one will believe me. My husband, who loves me, will not believe me; and he has treated me accordingly. What have I done to you that you should think yourself authorized to inflict such a public affront on me, for, if it isn't public yet, it will be to-morrow.

NOURVADY.

I have already told you: I love you.

LIONNETTE.

And this, then, is your fashion of proving your love?

NOURVADY.

If I had had any other at my disposal, I should have employed it. I love you (*changing his tone, and approaching her*). I have loved you madly for years. (*She recoils involuntarily from the movement of* NOURVADY.) Fear nothing: I dishonour you, perhaps, in the eyes of others, but I respect you; and you are sacred to me. If ever you are mine, it will only be with your consent; that is, when you will have said, "I return your love." I know well all the kinds of love one can buy! It is not for a love such as that I ask: you would not give it to me, and I do not wish for it from you. You are beautiful; I love you; and you have a great grief, a trouble, a common-place preoccupation, beneath your consideration, that one of your race and character ought never to know. On account of what? On account of some bank notes; of a few hundred pounds that you are in want of; and that I have in such profusion that I know not what to do with them. This grief—this annoyance—may cause you to lose your repose; may cost you your beauty—even your life; for you are a woman who would die in the face of an obstacle that you could not conquer. I have what is wanted to dispel this grief and care. I do it, therefore. Was it necessary to ask your permission? If I had seen your horse running away with you, should I have asked your permission to help you? I should have rushed to your horse's head and saved you, or he would have passed over my body. If I had saved your life, and survived, you would, perhaps, have loved me for that heroic act: if I had been killed, you would certainly have been sorry, and have wept for me. I have not exposed my life in saving you as I have done: I have not accomplished an act of heroism, I have only done a thing that was very easy for me; but I could not control the circumstances.

LIONNETTE.

Ah! Well, your devotion led you astray, Sir; and if I am in your house, it is to call upon you to repair—before it be irremediable—the harm you have done.

NOURVADY.

It is out of my power to do anything myself. I have expressly employed this method because I knew it to be the only one, and irremediable. It would be now necessary that your creditors should consent to take back their bills, and give back their money. Do you think they would consent to that?

LIONNETTE.

This, then, is what you said to yourself: This woman that I respect, esteem, and love, I am going first to compromise and dishonour her in the eyes of everybody; I am going to make her despised, insulted, and turned out of doors by her husband; and, the first emotion over, she will have nothing left to choose; she will take up her part, and will then be mine.

NOURVADY.

I did not reflect at all. It did not please me at all that the tradespeople should have the power of hunting and humiliating you. I paid them. I did not wish you to be sorrowful; I could not endure to see you poor. It is a fancy, like any other, and I am willing to take the consequences of my fancy. If you had been in my place you would have done what I have done.

LIONNETTE.

No! If I were a man and pretended to love an honest woman, whatever might come of it, I would respect her dignity and the proprieties of the society in which she moves.

NOURVADY.

Is it really a woman of your superiority who speaks of the proprieties of society? Are not women like you above all that? Was I to come delicately and hypocritically to offer your husband the sum he stood in need of? "Arrange your affairs, my dear friend; you can give me back that trifle when you are able." I should certainly have acted like that if I had not loved you; loving you, ought I to do it, that is to say, to speculate upon your gratitude, upon the impossibility of your husband discharging his debt, and upon fresh and unavoidable necessities? That is a course that would have been unworthy of him, of me, and of you. No, you know it well, the proprieties and dignity are nothing any longer, when passion or necessity predominates. Did your grandmother respect the dignity of her daughter when she gave her up to a prince?

LIONNETTE.

Sir!...

NOURVADY.

You do not fear words! There they are, those words, saying quite well all they have to say. Why do you rebel against them? Did your husband respect the dignity of his mother, the traditions of his family, the proprieties of the society in which he moved, when he issued a public summons to that irreproachable mother, to enable him to marry you? And you, yourself, while following your mother's counsel, did you say to that man: "My dignity is entirely opposed to marrying you under those circumstances, disowned, repulsed, disgraced by your mother"? Ah! well, I too, if I had met you when you were a young girl, I should have loved you as I love you now; and if my father had wished to prevent my marrying you, I should have acted like the Count. I envy him the sacrifice he was able to make for you, and that I can never make now.

LIONNETTE (*half mockingly, half sincerely*).

It may be so, but now it is too late. I am no longer open to marriage, and, unfortunately for you, I have no longer a mother.

NOURVADY.

But you may become a widow.

LIONNETTE.

Then, you really hate the Count?

NOURVADY.

Yes, almost as much as I love you.

LIONNETTE.

And you would like to prove it to him?

NOURVADY.

That is the second of my dreams. In the service that I rendered you, I knew perfectly well the insult I should inflict upon him, and much as I counted on your visit here, I was waiting in my house first for that of Mr. Godler and Mr. Trévelé, whom I had left expressly at your house yesterday until the Count returned home.

LIONNETTE.

How agreeable and convenient it is to be open and sincere and to play your cards so openly. Ah, well, sir, if my husband has not yet sent his two friends, it is because he wishes first to send you your money. He is gone in search of it.

NOURVADY.

He will not find it.

LIONNETTE.

I shall find it myself, without the ignominy which you anticipated. The Count will make a public restitution of the sum that you advanced in private, and will add to that restitution all that is required to make you justify your hatred.

NOURVADY.

He will strike me?

LIONNETTE.

That is not at all doubtful.

NOURVADY.

And I will kill him.

LIONNETTE.

That is not quite certain; he is courageous. A man who has no fear of death for himself, has a steadier hand to give it to another.

NOURVADY.

Pray for him; in the first place, it is your duty as a wife, and in the next, my death will be a fortunate event for you, indeed—a very good thing.

LIONNETTE.

In what way?

NOURVADY.

Because, having no relations, not a single true friend in this world, as is only to be expected in a millionaire like me; because, loving you as you deserve to be loved, in life and in death, I have made my will, in which I have said that you are the loveliest and purest woman I have ever met; that your husband, who will kill me, has unjustly suspected you, and that I entreat you, in compensation for the suspicion of which, my admiration and my esteem have involuntarily been the cause, to graciously accept for your son all that I possess, notwithstanding that I also detest that son.

LIONNETTE.

Why?

NOURVADY.

Because that child is the living proof of your love for your husband.

LIONNETTE (*aside*).

Alas! The child proves nothing. (*Aloud*) Never mind, all that is not ordinary, and you would, perhaps, finish by convincing me—with your death—provided that all this be true. If it be not true, it is well concocted.

NOURVADY.

Why should I deceive you? And what would you like me to do with my fortune if I die? What good would it be to me without my life, and in life what should I do with it without you? Whereas, if I die, my will is there by the side of the title deeds of proprietorship of this house, which you would only have had to sign if you had consented to be its owner during my life (*he points to a cabinet at the bottom of the room*), and your pocket money is here (*he shows the coffer*).

LIONNETTE.

Ah! yes, it is true. The famous million! There lies the temptation of the present hour. The tabernacle of the golden calf. Ah! well, let me look at it.... After all you have told me, who knows? perhaps, your god will convert me.

(*She walks towards the coffer, of which she opens the principal side. The gold contained in it is scattered all over the open panel.*)

LIONNETTE (*looking at the gold*).

It is certainly grand; like all which has power. There is contained ambition, hope, dreams, honour, and dishonour; the perdition and the salvation of hundreds—of thousands—of creatures, perhaps: it has no power for me. If I had loved my husband, I should, probably, take this million to save him: that would be one of the thousand base acts that one is called upon to commit in the name of true love. But, decidedly, I love no one and nothing. (*Shutting the coffer violently.*) Fight each other; kill each other; live or die, I am indifferent towards you both. You have both insulted me—each in your own way, and, always, in the name of love! Ah! if you only knew how what you call love becomes more and more odious to me. But, to make me believe in love, show me the man who respects that which he loves! I love you; that is to say, you are beautiful, and your flesh tempts me. It is to that temptation that I owed the husband who outrages me; it is to that temptation that I owe the insult that you have inflicted on me. A prince was not able to resist what he, too, called his love for a pretty girl; and I owe my existence to that so-called love! I must suffer on account of that; and, perhaps, in my turn, sell myself always on account of that! And that father dared not love me openly; me, his daughter; himself, a king! But, at least, he sometimes pressed me to his heart in secret: he wept; for he, too, suffered! Holding my head between his hands, he said to me,—he is the only one who ever said it to me,—"Be a virtuous woman always; it is the foundation of all good. Do you understand me?" And I believed him, and wished to be a virtuous woman, as he asked me to be; and it leads me to what? To be treated like one of the worst of creatures by him to whom I have remained faithful. And there is that man who insults me by his offer! His father made many millions by his bank; and he, the son, would like to buy me with them while I am yet young, be it understood. Why not? But, dear Sir, I am born of desire and corruption: they gave me no heart. With what, then, do you expect me to love you? I had no esteem for my mother: you do not know what it is not to esteem one's mother! My husband is an inexperienced, an idle, an unsophisticated man, who ought to have guided me; who did not know how; and whom I will never see any more. That is what I have come to. As to my son, I needed help, I took him in my arms yesterday, and he said to me, "I like better to go and play." Ah, well! let him get on without maternal dishonour. It will be a novelty in the family, and that will be my last luxury. It matters not. Amongst all this impurity and all these errors, there came on the scene, all of a sudden, one of the first gentlemen in the world; and his coming changed everything. I have royal blood in my veins. I shall never belong to you. Adieu! (*She goes towards the door at the back. Two violent and quick rings are heard at the bell of the entrance.*) What can that be?

NOURVADY.

A visitor who has made a mistake (*ringing*). Wait a moment! (*The Footman appears.*) Who is that?

THE FOOTMAN.

There are several men ringing at the door, but we have not opened it.

(*During this time* LIONNETTE *has covered herself with her veils.*)

NOURVADY.

Very well! Do not open it.

(*Two blows of a hammer are given on the hall door; after a little while, two more.*)

A VOICE (*from outside*).

For the third time, open.

LIONNETTE (*who has gone to look through the curtains of the window*).

My husband! With these men. Ah! this is complete.

NOURVADY.

Conceal yourself here. (*He shoves the door at the right.*)

LIONNETTE (*beyond herself with passion*).

I conceal myself! What do you mean? Who do you take me for? I have done no harm. All those people there are mad, decidedly. I want to see them quite close. (NOURVADY *goes to lock the door at the back.* LIONNETTE *has pulled off her veils, torn the fichu that was on her shoulders, and unrolled her hair by shaking her head.*) It was when I was like this that my husband thought me most beautiful! It is well, at least, that he should see me once more as he used to like to see me. Am I really beautiful like this?

NOURVADY.

Ah! yes; beautiful indeed.

LIONNETTE.

And you love me?

NOURVADY.

Very deeply.

LIONNETTE.

And all your life will be devoted to me?

NOURVADY.

All my life.

LIONNETTE.

You swear it to me?

NOURVADY.

On my word of honour.

(*He approaches her quickly. At that moment she stretches out her uncovered arms, and crosses them on her face; that she turns away.* NOURVADY *covers her arms with kisses.*)

A VOICE (*outside the door that* NOURVADY *has shut*).

Open!

NOURVADY.

Who are you?

THE VOICE.

In the name of the law.

NOURVADY.

I am in my own house. I refuse.

JOHN (*from outside*).

Break open that door.

LIONNETTE.

The coward!

THE VOICE.

It is I who give orders here, and I only. For the last time, will you open the door?

NOURVADY.

No!

THE VOICE.

Force that door.

NOURVADY (*to* LIONNETTE).

Tell me that you love me.

LIONNETTE.

Ah! yes, I love you; as he has driven me to it.

(*During these words the door was violently shaken, and it opens with a great noise.*)

SCENE III.

THE SAME PERSONS, JOHN, THE COMMISSARY OF POLICE, his SECRETARY, TWO AGENTS.

By an involuntary movement LIONNETTE *places herself on the side opposite to that on which she was with* NOURVADY. *In this way they become separated.* NOURVADY *walks in front of the* COMMISSARY OF POLICE. LIONNETTE *seats herself upon the couch, one arm half supported on the back of the couch, the other upon the little table which is there. Her three-quarters' profile is turned towards the audience in an attitude of anger and defiance at what is going on.* JOHN *points her out to the* COMMISSARY, *and wants to run towards her. The* COMMISSARY *stops him.*

THE COMMISSARY.

By virtue of an official mandate, I am required to come at the request of Count Victor Charles John de Hun, who is here, to prove the clandestine presence of the Countess Lionnette de Hun, wife of the said Count Victor Charles John de Hun, in the house of Mr. Nourvady, and to establish according to law the offence of adultery.

NOURVADY.

Sir!

THE COMMISSARY.

You will please be silent, sir, and reply only to my questions, if I have any to put to you. (*To* JOHN.) This gentleman is, I believe, Mr. Nourvady, whom you accuse of being an accomplice with your wife?

JOHN.

Yes.

THE COMMISSARY (*to* LIONNETTE).

Do you deny that, madam?

LIONNETTE.

No. I am, indeed, the legitimate wife of that gentleman, and Countess de Hun, alas!

THE COMMISSARY (*to an Agent*).

See that no one enters here! (*To the Secretary.*) Sit down and write. (*The Secretary sits down and prepares to write.*)

NOURVADY (*to* THE COMMISSARY).

But really, sir?

THE COMMISSARY.

I am Commissary of Police in your district; here are my insignia, sir. (*He shows one end of his scarf; dictating to his Secretary*). Having betaken ourselves to one of the residences of Mr. Nourvady....

LIONNETTE.

That is not correct, sir! Mr. Nourvady is not here in his own house, but in mine; this house and all that is in it belongs to me. Be kind enough to open this cabinet at your left and you will find there my title-deeds of ownership, which prove what I am stating.

THE COMMISSARY (*to one of his Agents*).

Open it. (*The Agent gives him all the papers that he finds in the cabinet.* THE COMMISSARY *reads them over.*) These papers are not quite according to law; it is a purchase made in your name but you have not ratified it, and your signature is wanting. (*While he is speaking he carries the papers to* LIONNETTE.)

LIONNETTE (*taking the papers and signing*).

There it is, and as the Count de Hun and I were married under the act of separation of property, and, as he legally gave me the right of acquiring and disposing of my property, I do not know what he wants here, in my house.

JOHN (*menacing her*).

Madam!

THE COMMISSARY.

Silence, sir, I beg of you. (*Dictating.*) We presented ourselves at the house which was indicated to us as one of the residences of Mr. Nourvady. Our visit was foreseen, and an order had been given to the servants to open the door to no one. After three legal summonses on our part, and three refusals on the part of the persons shut up in a room on the first floor, we broke open the door, and found in this room a man and woman, recognized to be Mr. Nourvady and the Countess Lionnette de Hun. The said lady, when we attributed to Mr. Nourvady the ownership of the house, formally declared to us that she was the owner of the house in which we found her, and furnished proofs of the same; also, she affirmed that Mr. Nourvady was paying her a visit there.

JOHN.

Add, if you please, sir, that I have disowned all participation in the ownership of this house, acquired without my consent, and by illegitimate means, which will be proofs of the charge of guilt.

THE COMMISSARY (*to the Secretary*).

Record the declaration of the Count de Hun. (*Dictating.*) After the refusal that was given to us, first by the servants of the house and then by Mr.

Nourvady.... You were the one, sir, were you not, who refused to open this door? (*He turns towards* Nourvady.)

Nourvady.

Yes, sir.

The Commissary.

After the refusal given and repeated three separate times by Mr. Nourvady, to open the door of the room where he was shut up with the Countess de Hun, although, according to the declaration of this lady, he was not in his own house, but her's, and, therefore, under the circumstances, she alone had a right to command there—after these repeated refusals, we found nothing to furnish us with convincing proofs of the charge that the complainant wished us to establish.

(*While speaking,* The Commissary *has run his eye over the stage, looking at the furniture, and lifting up the screens that separated the drawing room from other rooms.*)

John.

The presence of my wife in this house is sufficient to prove the crime.

The Commissary.

No, sir.

John.

In a case like this the intention is enough.

The Commissary.

We are not here to judge according to intentions, but to state according to facts.

JOHN (*picking up* Lionnette's *veils*).

What more do you require than this triple veil, which proves that my wife has come here concealing her face, as I saw, in short, for I followed her? A strange manner to enter her own house, since she maintains it to be her's. (*Pointing to* Lionnette.) Look at this, sir; what more do you require?

THE COMMISSARY.

Be as calm as possible, sir; the law will do its duty, however painful it may be. (*He dictates.*) Still, the attitude and bearing of the Lady de Hun, at the moment of our entrance, was at least suspicious. Her hair was half falling on her shoulders.

NOURVADY (*to* THE COMMISSARY).

Be good enough to note, sir, that at this point of your accusation I interrupted you, and that I affirmed most emphatically and on my word of honour the complete and perfect innocence of the Countess Lionnette de Hun, whose honour, whatever the appearances may be, should not be doubted for a moment.

LIONNETTE (*very calm at first, but gradually exciting herself to frenzy*).

And I, in the face of the scandal that my husband wished to create, and, though appreciating the motive of Mr. Nourvady's affirmation, which it is every honourable man's duty to make who wishes to save a woman's honour, I declare it false; and the facts that the law cannot prove I declare absolutely true. Mr. Nourvady was shut up here with me, by my wish, because he was, because he is, my lover.

JOHN (*running towards her*. THE COMMISSARY *puts himself between them.*)

Madam!

LIONNETTE.

Whatever may be the punishment of the adulteress, I merit it. (*To the Secretary, who hesitates.*) Write, sir, I have not finished. Write. (*She rises, and walks to the table where the Secretary is writing.*) So that there may not, by any possibility, be any mistake in the scandalous trials that will follow this scene, and in order that my husband may not have to accuse himself of casting upon me an unjust and hasty suspicion, I declare that not only have I given myself to Mr. Nourvady because I loved him, but because he is rich and I am poor; that after having ruined my husband I sold myself, so incapable was I of bearing poverty. The price of my fall is there: a million in gold struck expressly for me! My husband, there, was right yesterday, when he treated me like a prostitute. I am one, and very happy to be so. And if what I have told you does not convince you; if proofs are necessary, there they are! (*She steeps her bare arms in the gold, and throws handfuls of it all round her. To* JOHN.) And you, sir, if you are in want of money, take some; after the baseness that you commit at this moment, there remains only this for you to do.

JOHN (*going towards her; she looks in his face*; JOHN *falls on a chair*.)

Madam!... Ah!

LIONNETTE (*to* NOURVADY.)

And now do you believe that I am entirely yours?

JOHN.

In the face of the insolence and audacity of the accused, I require her immediate arrest.

THE COMMISSARY.

I know the rights that the law gives me, and the duties that I have to fulfil. All that has been said has been recorded in the accusation; I limit my office to that. (*To* NOURVADY.) As you are not in your own house, sir, you can retire; only as the avenue is full of people in front of the principal entrance, leave the house by this exit: one of my agents will join you, in order that the policeman may allow you to pass. (*He points to the left.* NOURVADY *bows to* LIONNETTE *and goes out by the left, passing in front of* JOHN, *who, standing with his arms folded, pretends not to see the provoking salute* NOURVADY *gives him*.)

THE COMMISSARY (*to* LIONNETTE).

With regard to you, Madam, as you are in your own house, enter, I beg of you, into your apartment, and if you wish to go out, do not go till some time after our departure, when there will be no longer inquisitive persons outside, and you will be sure not to be insulted.

LIONNETTE.

Thank you, sir.

(*She goes out by the door at the right*).

THE COMMISSARY (*to* JOHN).

I am going to deliver my report to the Judge. You have ten days to withdraw your complaint, sir—a complaint that perhaps you were very wrong to bring. That woman accuses herself too much. I believe her to be innocent. Go out of this house before me, sir; the people saw us come in together, and if we go out in the same way they will recognise you as the husband, and they might say disagreeable things to you. The French people do not approve of husbands who surprise their wives by the appearance of a Commissary of Police. I have the honour to wish you good morning.

(JOHN *bows to him and goes away*. THE COMMISSARY *comes back and sits down near his Secretary, to complete the last formalities*.)

ACT III.

The same decorations as in the first Act.

Scene I.

JOHN, GODLER, TRÉVELÉ.

(Godler *is sitting down*, Trévelé *standing*. John *is walking about in great agitation.*)

Godler.

And then?

John (*sitting down*).

Then, just as I was going to start for my sister's house, and everybody thought me gone, for I had no wish to sleep in this house, suddenly I was seized with the idea of concealing myself, and following my wife if she went out, so as to convince myself, and if she deceived me to disgrace her publicly. This morning I saw her go out veiled, take a cab, and alight at that house in the Champs Elysées. It was very clear. I went to fetch a Commissary of Police, who lives close by that house. He hesitated at first, but the fear of a greater misfortune, of a crime that I was resolved to commit, decided him to go; and on the refusal of Mr. Nourvady to open the door, they forced it open.

Trévelé.

And the Countess was there?

John.

Yes.

Trévelé.

With Nourvady?

John.

Yes.

GODLER (*after a little while*).

And you are convinced?...

JOHN.

Her hair undone, her arms bare, her dress-body opened! And such effrontery! such impudence! (*Rising, and putting his head in his hands.*) I witnessed it, I witnessed it. That man has done all in his power to exonerate her, to save her. He has given his word of honour that there has never been anything between them. It was not through any gentlemanly feeling, for he who comes to your house, takes you warmly by the hand, and appropriates, steals, and buys your wife, such a one has nothing of the true gentleman in him. But I do not know why I mention that man! After all, it is not he who is guilty; he has done his work as a man, as we have all done, and as we all do. He has met a beautiful creature, coquettish, fond of luxury, ruined, heartless, destitute of womanly feeling; heedless of her good name, her husband, or her child; without the least gratitude, or the least remembrance, even, of all I have done for her. He has offered to buy her, and she has consented. He has paid her a million; that is dear;—for what is a woman who sells herself really worth? As to me, I paid her with my name, with my mother's death and curse, that is still dearer. My mother saw clearly: she is avenged. I have no right to complain.

(*He sits down weeping, his head in his hands.*)

GODLER (*much moved*).

My poor old friend!

JOHN.

I beg your pardon. It is not to tell you all this that I have asked you to come here; but, after all, I have no one else now. Here am I, alone in the world. You are my friends—you have said so at least; and then again you did not come to my house to take her away, did you? Never mind, let us try to put my ideas a little in order. I do not know very well what I am about, you can understand that. However, you are convinced that I am an honest man? That is the reason I wanted to see you. You must tell me that you esteem me still. I may have been easily smitten, very stupid. I was so young then! Alas! I feel a hundred years old to-day. I may have been foolish to marry a creature unworthy of me; but you believe me, you know me incapable of all connivance with her; you feel certain that I have no hand in all this disgusting money affair? and when I have gone away, when I am dead, for it will certainly kill me in one way or another, you will take care to say, to affirm strongly, to swear to it even, that I was ignorant of the whole thing. I shall have lost my mother, my faith, my fortune, my life, for that woman; so be it, but at least I have preserved my honour!

GODLER.

Rely on us, my dear friend, and understand that we think you the most upright man in the world; that we esteem you for your honourableness, and sympathise with you in your great misfortune.

(TRÉVELÉ, *on his part, takes John warmly by the hand.*)

TRÉVELÉ (*aside*).

Poor fellow!

JOHN.

Then, you understand why I have raised this scandal instead of provoking the man. If I had been killed, a suspicion would always have rested on me. Mr. Nourvady paid the debts of my wife; they would have said that I did not find this enough, that I had asked for more, that he had refused me, that then I had quarrelled with him, that he had killed me, and that he had done right. If, on the contrary, I had killed him, they would have said worse things still; that I had waited until he had paid all household debts and had given my wife a fortune (for she has a splendid mansion), a million for her own use; and having arranged all that, and after all these disgraceful artifices, I had killed this generous lover; and that this was my way of settling with my creditors, and setting up my establishment again. This is why I have acted in this way. I wanted to raise an unmistakable scandal, well-spread abroad, from which it would be reported that she is a wretch and I an honest man ... and besides, before doing anything else, I must pay back his money.

GODLER.

According to the light in which you place the situation, I understand now what, with the habits of our set, I did not take in directly; from the point of view in which you place the thing, you have nothing else to do,—whatever may happen.

JOHN.

What do you mean by whatever may happen?

GODLER.

We never know! The human heart....

JOHN.

You believe me so weak, so much in love, and so base as to pardon this woman after what she has done! You know perfectly well that you despise me. It is my fault. My past weakness gives you the right to believe anything of me.

GODLER.

I believe nothing, I suppose nothing, but the whole thing appears to me very obscure, and passion, perhaps, has made you see things that do not exist. All I know is, that yesterday, in this house, Nourvady, before leaving us, spoke a long while in a low tone to the Countess. I heard nothing, but Trévelé was relating all sorts of nonsense to me, and I was supposed to be listening to it....

TRÉVELÉ.

Continue.

GODLER.

I looked unperceived at the Countess de Hun. Not only did she not listen with interest to her interlocutor, but two or three times her attitude and looks were indicative of anger. She threw something violently out of this window. I do not know what—a note, a trinket, a ring perhaps; and when Nourvady took leave of her, she said,—The insolent fellow! (*To* TRÉVELÉ.) Is it true?

TRÉVELÉ.

It is quite true....

JOHN.

She changed her mind afterwards. Night brings counsel: and she is only all the more guilty, as she knew very well what she was doing. Do not speak of her any more, I shall have to think enough about it for the rest of my life, which fortunately will not be long. At present I am going away, as I have no money, and must go and look for some.

GODLER.

My dear fellow!...

JOHN.

You understand, without my telling you, that I ask you for none, and that I should accept none. I confide in you because you are the only persons that I can consider at all as friends in our station, where one has so few; and what you do not give me out of friendship, you give me in esteem and compassion.

(GODLER *and* TRÉVELÉ *take him warmly by the hand.*)

TRÉVELÉ.

But the Countess, where is she?

JOHN.

She is, no doubt, in her house in the Champs Elysées.

TRÉVELÉ.

Then she will not come here?

JOHN.

Yes, she can come here. The house is hers; she can live here as much as she likes. It is I who am not at home here, and who come only to make my last preparations for departure.

Trévelé.

And Raoul? Your son?

John (*with a bitter laugh*).

Are you quite sure that he is my son?

Trévelé.

Do not let your anger mislead you.

John.

In any case he is the son of that woman; I do not wish to see him any more. He can live with her, that she may bring him up in her new life. He will avenge me one day. When he is twenty years old he will insult her. Or something else may occur. The tribunal which will pronounce our separation will order that the child shall be sent to college, or to boarding school, from which his mother will have no power to take him.

Trévelé.

At his age! He will be very unhappy.

John.

All the better for him. He will suffer at an earlier age—he will understand more easily.

A Servant (*entering*).

Mr. Richard.

John (*aside*).

It is not I who sent for him? Does he know anything?

Godler.

Would you like us to leave you?

John.

No. I have nothing to say that you may not hear.... unless you have something else to do.

TRÉVELÉ.

No, nothing. (*To* GODLER.) Nor you, have you?

GODLER.

I—no, nothing. (*To* TRÉVELÉ, *combing his whiskers and pulling forward his lock of hair*.) Florimonde is waiting for me.

TRÉVELÉ.

She is waiting for you with some one else. Be at ease, she will not be weary waiting for you.

SCENE II.

THE SAME PERSONS, RICHARD.

RICHARD (*in a low voice to* JOHN).

I know all, Count.

JOHN (*aloud*).

These gentlemen also....

RICHARD (*bowing*).

Your servant, gentlemen! (*To* JOHN.) I have received a note from the Countess, who begged me to go at once to the Commissary of Police and take a copy of the accusation, as the lawyer watching her interest, in the law proceedings which will take place. She has appointed an interview.

JOHN.

In what place?

RICHARD.

Here. She knew very well that I would not go anywhere else.

JOHN.

Then she is here?

RICHARD.

Yes.

JOHN.

Have you seen her?

RICHARD.

No; but the footman told me, and he is gone to inform her. I wanted to see you in the meantime.

JOHN.

And people already know it?

RICHARD.

Nothing; nothing at all. The Commissary has forbidden all communication with the newspapers, and it is neither you, nor Mr. Nourvady, nor we—is it not so, gentlemen? who would reveal the least circumstance in that sad affair. The servants of the house in the Champs Elysées know what took place, but they are ignorant of the name of the lady. The scandal will be great enough at the time of the law proceedings. It is useless to initiate the public beforehand.

JOHN.

Ah! Well, you can see the affair is very simple. The Countess and I were separated, or had a separation of property; now we have a separation of the body, and we shall see each other no more; that is the whole of it.

THE LADY'S MAID (*entering*).

The Countess de Hun sends me to say to Mr. Richard, that when he has finished speaking to the Count she will be glad to see him....

JOHN (*to the Lady's Maid*).

Say to the Countess that Mr. Richard will be with her in a few minutes. (*The Lady's Maid goes away.*) Ah! she has audacity. When a woman has once taken up the part of infamy and dishonour it is dreadful. (*To Richard.*) Tell her especially that she has nothing to fear, nothing to hope from me, of whom she will hear nothing more till we meet before the tribunal that will try our case. Good bye, my dear Mr. Richard; you are her lawyer and her friend; you ought, naturally and legally, to act in her cause. I shall think no less of you for all you will be called upon to say against me. Gentlemen, we can retire; give me a few minutes more.

(*All three go away.*)

SCENE III.

RICHARD, afterwards LIONNETTE.

RICHARD *is about to take up his hat. At the moment that he is thinking of entering* LIONNETTE'S *apartment, she appears.*

LIONNETTE.

I prefer to receive you here, my dear Mr. Richard, as we shall be left alone and uninterrupted. My room, and my private reception-room, are in disorder; they are packing my trunks—the servants are there, and we could not talk privately. The reason I called you just now was, that the Count might be aware that I was here, and that I was in a hurry to see you. Have you been kind enough to do what I asked you?

RICHARD.

Yes.

LIONNETTE.

Then I have nothing more to tell you?

RICHARD.

No. All that is then quite true?

LIONNETTE.

Nothing on earth can be truer.

RICHARD.

Notwithstanding yesterday?

LIONNETTE.

Events have progressed, and I preferred to have done with it at once. I was right. I am calmer now than I have ever been in my life. I know at last what I want, and where I am going. It is a great deal, whatever one may make of it. I have struggled hard against it, but it seems that I am doomed to end in being a courtesan. Truly, I do not feel any inclination that way. Frivolous, extravagant, but never depraved. However, they willed it; it was inevitable; it was ordained; it was hereditary. My dear Mr. Richard, I have to ask you for some information, because I am still a little inexperienced in my new profession; but from the moment one begins to do those things, they must be done openly, is it not so? Ah! well, here are the title-deeds of some property I have acquired.

RICHARD.

Dearly?

LIONNETTE.

Yes, very dearly.

RICHARD.

And the price is paid?

LIONNETTE.

It is paid.

RICHARD.

Is it true?

LIONNETTE.

Paid or not paid, here are the title-deeds. (*Putting them on the table, and beginning to totter.*) Then I possess, too, over and above all my paid debts —for they are paid—I am possessor, also, of a million in gold, quite new: it is superb to look at.

RICHARD.

Sit down, you look as if you were going to fall. You are quite pale; the blood has rushed to your heart.

LIONNETTE (*with a great effort*).

Do not be afraid, I am quite strong. I cannot eternally keep a million in gold ... however beautiful it may be ... it is an incumbrance, and then it might be stolen from me ... and money ... is everything in this world! Without reckoning that in cash this million will yield nothing ... and I want it to produce something.... I should like, then, to place it out in the best way possible. You must place it for me in safety, where it cannot be touched, like the little income that remains to the Count; so that I, too, may not want bread in my old age. I am such a spendthrift. I count entirely on you for that.

RICHARD.

And where is this million?

LIONNETTE.

It is over there, in my house, the house that I ... bought—in a coffer that I have even forgotten to shut; that is to say ... there are pieces of gold lying in all directions ... on the table ... on the carpet. The Commissary of Police opened his eyes!... If the footmen have taken some, say nothing about it.... I am rich ... for there is also in a cabinet a will of Mr. Nourvady, who, in the event of his death, leaves me all his fortune: forty millions. That is worth something! But death is like everything else in this world, it must not too surely be reckoned on.

RICHARD (*aside*.)

Poor creature!

LIONNETTE.

You already have my power of attorney, from the time that my affairs got into confusion. It will enable you to take possession of my house and of my capital during my absence. There ought also to be some jewels, a great many jewels, in the drawers; I have not the least idea which, however; I have never opened them—I have not even thought of them! You will deposit them all in your house I do not want them in travelling ... and then, I shall have plenty of others given to me—now; I shall have all I can wish for given to me.

RICHARD.

And you are going away with Mr. Nourvady?

LIONNETTE.

We start this very day.

RICHARD.

It is positively arranged?

LIONNETTE.

I think so; I have not seen him again, but I want absolutely to start to-day.

RICHARD.

And where will you meet?

LIONNETTE.

I suppose they will come for me here.

RICHARD.

Quite openly?

LIONNETTE.

Quite openly; at least, if they have not already had enough of me ... that may happen ... anything may come to pass.... That would be strange.

RICHARD.

Do you love Mr. Nourvady, then?

LIONNETTE (*hoping to deceive* RICHARD).

Madly, and for a long time past. I struggled against it. And then, candidly, in the position in which I was, it was the only thing to do.

RICHARD.

And your husband?

LIONNETTE (*sincere*).

Oh! he! that is another thing; I hate him ... oh, yes! I hate him *well* ... without doubt....

RICHARD.

And your child?

LIONNETTE.

I see at what you are aiming, my dear Mr. Richard ... you want to touch my tender feelings. Feel my hands, they are cold; listen to my voice, it does not tremble; if you put your hand on my heart, you would feel that I have not one pulsation more than ordinarily. You still hope there is some remedy for what has happened ... there is none ... there can never be any. If there were any I should reject it. Would you like me to open my heart to you? I merit what has happened. I often condemned my mother, because the guilty always accuse some one else of the faults that they commit; but I am no better than she was. There is too great a mixture in me, and I should be foolish to attempt to discover what I am. I am simply and logically what I was destined to be. I shall not be the first woman who was proud of her disgrace, especially in these times; and what difference will that make to the world? I ought to have been economical or ugly! These two men who hate each other, and are equally resolved to be the ruin of me, are yet better than I, for they love, though one suffers and the other desires; whereas I desire nothing more, I can suffer no more, and this disclosure of affairs will appear quite natural to those who knew me. It is horrible; it is monstrous ... it is all that, and I tell it to you because I have no one now to deceive, thank God! And, apart from that, I am going into vice that I like no better than anything else, as I entered into marriage and motherhood, without considering why. I have no heart! no heart! that is at the bottom of it all. A creature of luxury and pleasure. You ask me, then, why I do not kill myself—why I do not put an end to myself—that is the word? That would be done more quickly, and would simplify everything. Yesterday I was ready to die to avoid dishonour. To-day, what good would it do? I am dishonoured. What do you want me to destroy in myself? Nothing has any more life in me, and it seems that I can still bestow pleasure, love—happiness may be. You say to yourself that all that is impossible, because you call to mind your mother, your wife, your children. Yes, there are, indeed, mothers, wives, children ... and, again, there are some beings who have the same forms, and bear the same names, but who are not in any degree the same thing. What do you want still to know?

RICHARD.

I do not dispute; only embrace your child for the last time.

LIONNETTE.

Why disturb him? he is playing no doubt.

RICHARD.

I am going to look for him.

LIONNETTE.

No, I beg of you. (RICHARD *walks towards the room.*) I do not wish it. (THE FOOTMAN *appears.*)

THE FOOTMAN.

Mr. Nourvady would like to know if the Countess de Hun can receive him.

LIONNETTE (*in a natural tone.*)

Certainly! (*To* RICHARD.) Good bye, my dear Mr. Richard ... I will write if I have any instructions to give you. My kind regards to your wife ... if she knows nothing yet.

RICHARD.

Do not remain long here, that will be more prudent.

LIONNETTE.

I am going away directly.
(THE FOOTMAN *lets* NOURVADY *pass, and goes away.*)

NOURVADY.

You excuse me, Madam?

LIONNETTE.

For what?

NOURVADY.

For coming here to look for you.

LIONNETTE.

Wherever I may be, have you not the right to come there; I was waiting for you. I said so, a moment ago, to Mr. Richard, who knows all.

RICHARD.

Good-bye, Countess.

LIONNETTE (*giving him her hand with an involuntary and visible emotion*).

Adieu, my dear Richard.

RICHARD (*bowing coldly to* NOURVADY).

Sir.... (*He goes away.*)

Scene IV.

LIONNETTE, NOURVADY, afterwards RAOUL.

LIONNETTE.

You appear quite distressed.

NOURVADY.

It is on your account.

LIONNETTE.

I thought nothing ever troubled you! It is the scene of this morning that has unnerved you.

NOURVADY.

In the first place....

LIONNETTE.

The fact is that you were hurt at the way in which the Commissary entered; and your millions were powerless. As to me, I am quite myself again. You love me still?

NOURVADY.

You ask me that?

LIONNETTE.

One never knows. The heart is so changeable. You see, this morning I did not love you; it is not five o'clock, and I love you. (*She rings twice violently.*)

NOURVADY.

You are feverish; you, too....

LIONNETTE.

That will go off.... (*To the Lady's Maid, who has entered*) Bring me my things to go out.

NOURVADY.

Is your husband in this house?

LIONNETTE.

Yes.

NOURVADY.

Have you seen him?

LIONNETTE.

No.

NOURVADY.

It is, nevertheless, to see you, that he has come back here.

LIONNETTE.

No more than that I came here to meet him. We were living here; we are both going away, each his own way. We come to get what we want. It is evident that he and I would very much prefer, at this moment, to be somewhere else. It is you who ought not to be here; but, since this morning, it is strange we are all in places where we ought not to be. (*To the Lady's Maid, who comes back.*) That will do; put them down there.

(*The maid, puts down a hat, gloves, and a travelling cloak, and goes away.*)

NOURVADY.

I went back to your house, hoping to find you there. You had gone away. I supposed you were here. The servant who announced me, and who, evidently, knows nothing of all that has happened....

LIONNETTE.

No one knows anything about it except the parties interested.

NOURVADY.

The servant asked me if he were to announce me to the Count or Countess de Hun. It was in that way that I knew that your husband was here at the same time as you. I had a strong inclination to say to the man: Announce me to your master.

LIONNETTE.

What could you have to say to him now?

NOURVADY.

He came to look for you in my house: I come to look for you in his. You are a woman; you do not understand certain insults.

LIONNETTE.

Do you think so?

NOURVADY.

That man forced my door; he even broke it. He insulted you before me, who love you.

LIONNETTE.

You must remember he loves me too: that is his excuse.

NOURVADY.

You defend him.

LIONNETTE (*while putting on her hat, mantle, and gloves*).

Ah! heaven help me, no! Well, what would you have said to him if they had announced you to him as you said, and he had received you? But I doubt if he would have received you after what is passed.

NOURVADY.

If he had refused to receive me, I should have burst open his door in my turn, and....

LIONNETTE.

Ah! I forbid you absolutely to provoke him at present.... If I were a widow through you ... or if he killed you, you would not be able to marry me ... and if, one day, we could legitimize the false position we are going to hold, I should be very glad of it. Let us trust to Providence, as my mother used to say. Apart from all that, I am ready.... Let us start!...

(*At the moment that she turns round to go out* RAOUL *enters, and throws himself into her arms to kiss her*.)

RAOUL.

Mamma!

LIONNETTE (*surprised and agitated*).

Ah! it is you. You frightened me!

RAOUL.

Kiss me.

LIONNETTE (*kissing him coldly*).

You think then of embracing me to-day. (*With a sigh*) It is rather late.

RAOUL.

Where are you going?

LIONNETTE.

I am going out.

RAOUL.

When are you coming back?

LIONNETTE.

I don't know.

RAOUL.

To-day?

LIONNETTE.

To-day.

RAOUL.

Take me with you.

LIONNETTE.

It is impossible.

RAOUL.

Why? It is such fine weather.

LIONNETTE.

I am going too far. I shall send you some toys, you may be sure.

RAOUL.

I like better going with you.

LIONNETTE.

Impossible, I tell you. Go now; let me pass.

RAOUL.

No!

LIONNETTE.

You must, my child.

NOURVADY (*very agitated and very impatient during this scene, walks from right to left to see if any one is coming.*)

Some one is coming.

LIONNETTE (*a little more harshly*).

Now, now, let me go.

RAOUL.

No. (*He puts himself in front of his mother.*)

NOURVADY (*taking the child by the arm, and throwing him far from him*).

Leave us alone, then!

(*The child totters, falls, and remains motionless.* LIONNETTE *stops, looks with stupor on what has passed, recoils, covers her face with her hands, utters a piercing cry, and rushes at* NOURVADY, *whom she seizes by the throat as if to strangle him.*)

LIONNETTE.

Miserable wretch!

NOURVADY (*whom she has struck on the shoulder, who feels himself getting exhausted, but who will not defend himself, with a feeble voice*).

You are hurting me.

LIONNETTE (*releasing him*).

Go away; go away! I shall strangle you. I shall kill you. My child! My child!

(*She utters several cries, and throws herself in despair upon the child.*)

RICHARD (*who has entered during this scene, to* NOURVADY).

Go away, sir, go away, in the name of heaven! Enough of such misfortunes, without that.

(*He makes* NOURVADY *go away.*)

RAOUL (*half raising himself up*).

There is nothing the matter ... Mamma.... Nothing, I assure you.

(LIONNETTE *on her knees, with* RAOUL'S *head on her breast, kissing him with rapture, sobbing without power to stop herself*).

RICHARD (*near her*).

Saved! You are saved!

LIONNETTE (*with sobs, tremulously accentuating every word*).

Yes, yes, yes, saved! (*To* RICHARD.) Ah! I was mad.... I was mad.... But when that man laid his hand on my child, it is awful what took possession of me! I do not know how it was I did not kill him. What is the use of a man struggling with a mother? For I am a mother. I am.... Oh! I felt it truly, from my heart, that that could never be. Richard, you guessed rightly; yes. Right-minded people guess rightly!... They want my father's letters; very well, they shall have them. You shall sell everything; you shall pay—you must give that man back his money;—there will be an end to it all. Go, and find my husband. (RICHARD *goes away.*) I want to see him before I die, for I am going to die, I feel it.

(*She lets her head fall upon the couch, and half loses consciousness.*)

RAOUL (*jumping upon the couch, taking his mother's head in his arms, and kissing it.*)

Mamma, mamma, mamma ... do not die, I beseech you.

LIONNETTE (*recovering consciousness*).

No, no, I shall live, for I love you!...

(*She covers him with kisses, and does not see* JOHN, *who enters with* RICHARD, *who is showing him the scene.* JOHN *starts back, comprehending nothing yet.* GODLER *and* TRÉVELÉ *look on and rejoin* JOHN, *who cannot take his eyes off the picture of the mother and her child.* RICHARD *touches* LIONNETTE'S *shoulder, who turns round and sees* JOHN.)

SCENE V.

LIONNETTE, JOHN, RAOUL, RICHARD, GODLER, TRÉVELÉ.

LIONNETTE *to* JOHN (*running to him and falling on her knees*).

Do not leave me any more. I will explain all to you. I understand, I see it all clearly now! I am innocent, I swear to you! I swear to you! I swear to you! We will live modestly in some quiet place, wherever you like. What difference does that make now that my child has awakened my soul in me?

(*She throws herself again on her son's neck*).

JOHN (*in the hands of* GODLER *and* TRÉVELÉ).

My friends, my friends, I am losing my senses!

GODLER.

You can, indeed, boast of having a true woman as a wife!

TRÉVELÉ (*touching him*).

Go and kneel at her feet.

(LIONNETTE *is sitting on the couch, supporting her son's head on her knees, and her head thrown back, in an attitude of weariness and contentment.* JOHN *throws himself on his knees before her, and kisses the hand she has free. She holds out the other to* RICHARD.)

LIONNETTE (*to* RICHARD).

It was just in time.

RICHARD.

Yes, the cry of a child! that is sufficient. When all is nearly lost, God's way is all-powerful.

JOHN.

I believe in you, and I love you.

LIONNETTE (*with a long sigh of joy*).

Ah! how happy I am!

GODLER (*wiping his eyes*).

How foolish I am, at my age!

TRÉVELÉ (*to* GODLER, *wiping his eyes, and trying to conceal his emotion*).

Bring forward your lock of hair.

CHATEAU DE SALNEUVE, *September*, 1880.

FINIS.

CPSIA information can be obtained
at www.ICGtesting.com
Printed in the USA
LVHW012321210423
745024LV00007B/137

9 781805 474432